Through the Eye
of the Needle

A Book of Poetry

Un libro de poesía

GLADE A. MYLER

 **Trafford** PUBLISHING® www.trafford.com
North America & international
toll-free: 1 888 232 4444 (USA & Canada)
fax: 812 355 4082

Contents

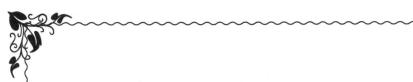

Preface

Words are magical when put together to create one of the many forms of communication. They help us to order our world, our universe which we are introduced to at birth. Although each word may serve a particular purpose when first used, over the years, words, through usage, take on additional meanings and nuances. In addition, words, if used too frequently, can become mere placeholders or slang, and even may lose meaning altogether. For example, the word *like* usually means "to enjoy or have an affinity for something," or it is used as a comparative word to show similarities among different things. Now it has become nothing more than a placeholder, in the common vernacular, when the communicator cannot think of another word to use. Such an occurrence saddens me since I have worked and studied language for many years. To have valuable words corrupted is anathema to those who are conservative and cherish the older speech patterns of the language, but I realize that language is a living thing that is always subject to change. This work contains many words used in the common way and, more often, in the original meaning, with a little twist in combination with other words to convey feelings and messages with universal meaning.

Words also carry their own poetry with them with natural rhythms and meter and, even, sometimes their own rhymes, such as words with onomatopoeia and alliteration. Many may question why my poems have no rhyme, but I believe that they do have rhyme, merely because rhyme is inherent in many words. Nevertheless, I have chosen not to compose poetry with the traditional rhyming schemes, but one will note that many of the Spanish poems carry the traditional meter schemes of Spanish poetry. If there is any traditional rhyme in any poems, it is only incidental and not intended.

Some of the individual poems were composed first in another language, primarily Spanish, and then translated and changed somewhat to become poems in English. There is one poem in Portuguese, which may not be obvious, but which was inspired while I was reading a work in Portuguese. Since Spanish is my second language (I have spoken for many years and have taught Spanish to English speakers as well as instructed Spanish-speaking attorneys about the American legal system), it has been the inspiration for many of my works. My Spanish has not been corrupted as much by common usage as has my English. It is my hope that each poem truly conveys to the reader my deep feelings and thoughts, whether in English or another language.

Many of my poems are written in the sonnet form with fourteen lines each. However, they are not in the traditional Elizabethan of Italian forms as are many of the older sonnets. They do not have rhyme, but most of the Spanish sonnets do have meter. I chose the sonnet form because when composing them I often did not have much time to capture the ideas which came to me and the sonnet is a shorter form allowing for brevity with power.

The title of this work, *Through the Eye of the Needle*, comes from a biblical reference when Jesus Christ was referring to the difficulty of a camel going through the eye of a needle, which in His day referred to some of the gates of Jerusalem. They were so small that camels would have to be unburdened of their cargos and then would have to get down on their knees to get through the gate. As a child, I often contemplated that metaphor and, in my naïveté, would wonder how it would be to gaze through the eye of a sewing needle and what the perspective would be on the other side. Could it be the Emerald City or a dark, dangerous enchanted forest? Some of these poems may serve to allow us to envision the other side of the eye of that sewing needle.

Each day, each season of the year, special occasions, and memorable moments are just some of the themes of my poems. My childhood in a rural setting and my later years at school and living in large metropolitan areas of this country have all contributed to these poems in some way. We are all an eclectic of our backgrounds and varied experiences. Such variations are the essence of existence and give rise to different perspectives on a certain theme. Age, hopefully, with its acquired wisdom, can reach back and give more meaning to the youthful experiences we all have shared. Perhaps this work will aid each of us to examine ourselves and strive to be better tomorrow than today and to share our experiences with those who may be struggling with the same roadblocks which we may have already overcome. My only desire with this work is to share with others those feelings and thoughts that have molded me and helped me to order this universe with its depravities, inhumanity, kindnesses, love, and finally, but most importantly, divinity.

Acknowledgments

I must express gratitude to the many who have assisted with this work in whatever way, especially the encouragement of friends and loved ones to complete this work and share it with others. I am indebted to the English, Languages and Philosophy, and Music Departments of Utah State University, as well as the Spanish Department of Indiana University for the education I received in literature and music, which has been invaluable in my lifetime and which has helped in the creation of many of my works. Incidentally, my law degree from Brigham Young University has provided an invaluable education in writing. Also, I would like to thank the Ash Canyon Poets of Carson City, Nevada, who tutored me in poetry for a number of years—particularly William Cowee, now deceased—for their encouragement and understanding. Most of all, I want to thank my devoted wife for her help in putting this work together and for her photography that is part of this work.

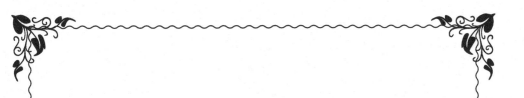

Cutting Strawberry Runners

In late spring brings certain
   trepidation, but resolve
to assist a new generation
   in sending down roots into
fertile soil carefully prepared
   by many long since
returned to earth beneath
   those tender shoots.

Older plants continue to
   produce succulent berries,
red, vibrant and enticing,
   while still sheltering
their vulnerable progeny.
   Yet, now each begins
imperceptibly to wilt in life—
   giving, but perilous sun.

In spite of mature vigor, all
   feel inevitable loss as runners
are meticulously severed,
   anchored and nourished
with anxious tears.

(Graduation Day)

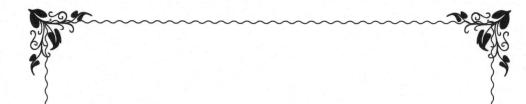

Pavane

—A meditation on Ravel's "Pavane for a Dead Princess"

Peace, after rain, flows like the notes
   from a melancholy flute as my mind
softly drifts into needful sleep after
   spontaneous waves of purging sorrow.

Yet the echo of that sweet melody I
   hear, like loving arms, encircles me
as gentle tears of grief for my dead
   princess soothes this saddened heart
now searching for lasting solace.

When acceptance finally comes,
   I seal my love with a tender kiss
to that forehead now still, and with
   a whisper of farewell, I longingly
await that glorious spring when we
   will again dance on velvet clouds
to the rhythm of this sweet pavane.

Opus in White Major

White on white brilliant as noonday sun
   radiates through crystalline windows,
reflecting sparkling snow gently blanketing
   a weary earth with welcome stillness.

Peace settles over all like transparent
   dew, as morning's grandeur bathes once
again nature's music in dazzling brightness.

Darkness flees before this celestial exhibit
   as warmth springs like soothing tears melting
the bosom of night now emitting rays pure
   as diamonds to spark frozen air into luminaries
falling into drifts, then disappearing into
   a symphony of white, intoned on the harps
and silver-toned violins of winter's morning.

"How Lovely is Thy Dwelling Place"

—Brahms, "German Requiem"

Las raras veces cuando se parte el velo
entre esta vida y el porvenir, se refleja
en las bellezas ocultas y escondidas
en cada nota de música celestial.

Mas, se quedan encarceladas y tristes
esperando otro instante de inspiración
cuando la musa toca la frente lista
para libertarlas a brotarse en gloria
y proveer esos momentos deliciosos
para los que tienen oídos para oír.

En tales ocasiones el ser conmovido
por la hermosura recién probada regresa
descontento y solemne a esperar con paciencia
otra ojeada más allá del velo esquivo.

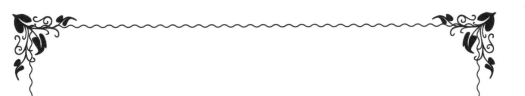

"How Lovely is Thy Dwelling Place"

—Brahms, "German Requiem"

There are rare occasions when the veil
 between this life and the hereafter parts
briefly to reveal the obscured and hidden
 beauties in each note of celestial music.

However, those beauties often remain sadly
 imprisoned awaiting the moment of inspiration
when the muse touches a brow prepared
 to liberate them, allowing them to blossom
gloriously creating wonderful melodies
 only for those who have ears to hear.

When these instances which bathe a soul in
 exquisiteness end, one must reverently, yet
reluctantly return, only to patiently await another
 glimpse beyond that ever mysterious veil.

"Peace Like a River"

Mirrors in still waters reflect the peace
   of creation silently, unnoticeably spinning
through the universe while the mists
   of the rivers converge into life-giving
clouds for parched earth awaiting salvation.

A lone, fallen leaf floating freely, aimlessly
   in time forms ripples interrupting the calm
momentarily and attracting a swimming
   bird anxious for another meal graciously
provided by the source of all benevolence.

"Eye hath not seen, nor ear heard,
   nor entered into the heart of man"
the treasures held in store for all
   who listen to the peace of a river.

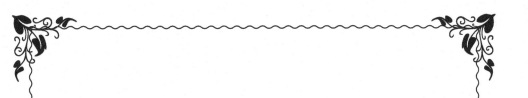

Feelings

With you cradled in my arms, love
    ebbs and flows from me to you
with contentment in each breath,
    as evident in your eyes sweetly
reflecting fragile trust and devotion
    planted within your tender breast.

Not wanting to disturb this fleeting
    tranquility, I hesitate only a few
precious moments, to treasure
    these delicate feelings of affection.

Unable to accept the inevitable end
    to this bit of welcome serenity, I close
my eyes, now wet with tears of longing
    for promised days of unending love.

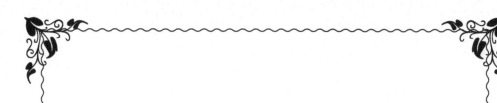

Sinfonía de mañana

Una mañana sosegada despliega el horizonte
con las nubes coloradas y cielo pintado azul.

Sólo algunas aves interrumpen esta maravilla
volando como apenas puntos moteando cañamazo
del artista lista para imprimir otro día especial.

Brisa sedosa acaricia los árboles y criaturas
comenzando las actividades de otro día, ignorantes
de la hermosura amplia de nueva aurora replandeciente.

Más bién, en pinturas y fotos los artistas congelan
tal prodigio a fin de preservarlo para días oscuros
sin felicidad cuando cielos gris reinan sin cesar.

Así, lucho con afán con esta mi pluma a captar
la esencia de las mañanas brillantes que por siglos han
inspirado la alma impresionante hasta moverla a lágrimas.

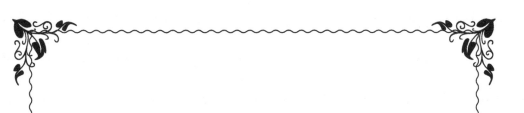

Morning Symphony

On a serene morning, the horizon displays
red clouds in a beautiful sky painted blue.

The only interruption to this breathtaking scene
are a few lone birds appearing like small dots on
the artist's canvas, ready to capture this moment.

A gentle breeze caresses the trees, and all
creatures, beginning their activities of the day, are
unaware of another exquisitely beautiful dawn.

Artists strive with paintings and photos to freeze
such a wonder, preserving it for those gray days without
much happiness, when sullen skies seem endless.

With great effort, I too attempt to seize with this pen
the essence of brilliant mornings which have for centuries,
inspired impressionable souls, moving them to tears.

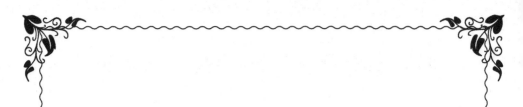

Jean Valjean

History disguised as poignant
    fiction reveals an inherent truth:

Deep from within the sordid
    labyrinth of inhumane excess
emerge saintly giants forged
    in the furnace of affliction
to remind mankind that we
    are endowed with innate worth,
to rally the forces of good and
    champion the inevitable struggle
against blind, cruel avarice.

Just as warm spring rain melts
    harsh winter's grip, so pure love
arises from the ashes of hatred
    and despair redeeming those
caught in the web of bitter revenge.

Only then can true beauty return
    as the flower of forgiveness,
transforming a world ripe for self-
    destruction and placating the
yearnings of each penitent soul.

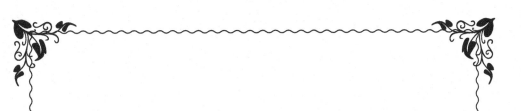

To the Forrest Gumps of the World

Some say heroes are not made from individual
circumstances, but from one's nurturing and
substance, when bravery comes naturally as
adrenaline shuts down self-preservation's cowardice.

Also, we know reasoning alone leaves many a battlefield
strewn with egos too proud to accept defeat and accomplish
those Good Samaritan rescue missions awaiting all of us.

Through perseverance and even stubbornness those
who have made themselves as humble, teachable
little children, become guardians for others who
have given up on life's seemingly futile struggles.

These saviors are strategically placed in our
lives to affect a rescue of the enduring part
of us, very often eroded by doubts and unbelief.

It only takes the resolute courageous determined
to succeed, in spite of the handicaps we all have,
to cause good to arise from the idiot in us all.

Nocturno Español

La música de una sinfornía de grillos de
*   verano produce nostalgia que me inunda*
tormentándome con ambivalencia hirviendo
*   hasta reventarse en un poema colorado.*

La noche con sus temores imaginados
*   me envuelve en sonido bello de castañuelas*
cencerreando a la serenata de Don Juan
*   desterrado y enamorado en balcón oculto.*

La Mancha me llama como una sirena sutil
*   aunque desconocida, sino por lectura*
deliciosa e ingeniosa de ese maestro fino
*   que ha tentado probar esa fruta efímera.*

Màs, pronto termina sueño extravagante
*   pero persiste el sabor dulce siempre.*

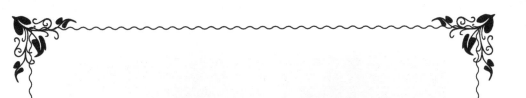

Spanish Nocturne

The music of a symphony of crickets
   in summer produces nostalgia which floods
me with seething storms of ambivalence
   which burst forth into a colorful poem.

Night with its imagined fears envelops
   me with the beautiful sounds of castanets
clicking to the serenade of Don Juan,
   exiled and lovesick on a cloaked balcony.

La Mancha calls to me like a cunning siren
   even though it is only known to me through
the ingenious and delicious text of that
   master who strove to taste the illusive fruit.

Suddenly, this flamboyant dream ends,
   but the sweet taste persists forever.

Scars

These scars I suffer serve
   to remind me of past
injuries now partially
   forgotten, but not buried.

If these scars encourage
   me, like the fierce winds
goad me to cover myself,
   and wait patiently for
merciful warming of spring,
   then I have triumphed.

It is in the surrendering to
   adversity and rationalizing
the causes of my misfortune
   is when I sadly fall short.

The instinct to survive is
   strong among all living
creatures, but the scars from
   storms and predators can
only be softened over time.

Yet, some day, after much
   contrition and humility, these
scars will surely be erased
   by the tender touch of divinity.

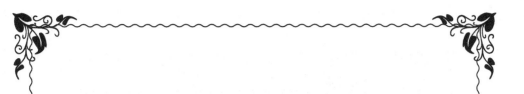

"Considerad los lirios del campo . . .

—ni aún Salomón con toda
su gloria se vistió como uno de ellos.:
(Mateo 6:28, 29)

Al contemplar esta maravilla llamada
  naturaleza se disuelven las muchas
preocupaciones que inquietan la alma,
  como la noche suaviza los remolinos.

El balance entre los elementos se
  refleja en el intercambio de las plantas
y los animales cuando respiran lo que
  el otro rechaza y, de cierto, disdeña.

El nacimiento de belleza en una flor
  de la pudrición de otros organismos
inspira asombro aún en cada persona
  empedernida por su propia importancia.

El cielo mismo entona este canto
  e instrumenta la sinfonía de la puesta
del sol al destacarse el azul
  entre nubes doradas y rosadas.

Con noche y la oscuridad, el silencio
  de sueño reina sobre el mundo
de la naturaleza encubriendo
  pesar de vivir en capullos de olvido.

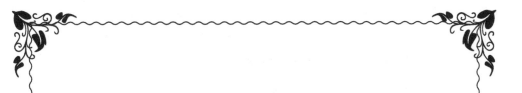

"Consider the lilies of the field . . .

even Solomon in all his glory was
not arrayed like one of these."
—Matthew 6:28, 29

Upon contemplating the many marvels
　　of nature, the frivolous cares of this world
which preoccupy our time and thoughts
　　dissipate, like night soothes the whirlwinds.

The delicate balance of the elements
　　is reflected in the interchange of plants
and animals as each breathes in what
　　the other rejects and, certainly, disdains.

The beauty of a newly-opened flower
　　born from the decomposition of other
matter inspires awe in all human beings,
　　even those hardened by self-importance.

As the sky also intones this natal song,
　　orchestrating the glorious setting of
the sun, the ethereal blue is enhanced
　　by dazzling gold and rose-colored clouds.

With night and darkness, the silence
　　of sleep rules the world, as a natural
blanket for grief and sorry, covering
　　us in cocoons of forgetfulness.

Metamorphosis

Longing to teach and warn from
   my experienced vantage point,
with ambivalent eyes I see him.

Among many spurts of hormonal
   activity and with a sponge-like mind,
he touches with his finger-eyes.

Stomach prone with palms supporting
   his chin, shoeless feet swinging freely,
in a rare, quiet moment, he pauses
   to contemplate a cocoon suspended
precariously under a teardrop leaf.

Too anxious to await the miraculous
   change, he bolts to other wonders
leaving the pupa to unavoidable perils,
   while he narrowly escapes the sting
of a bee frightened from his haste.

His mirthful childhood behind him,
   he ventures forth handsomely
dressed with a bow tie and tuxedo.

He stops, unaware of a now-empty
   chrysalis, to lean against a tree and
thoughtfully ponder the universe
   before him, as the splendid butterfly
slowly flutters with wings still damp
   and lights upon his youthful shoulder.

The realization that yesterday is
   gone brings a knowing tear burning
my cheek as I see both poised upon
   the threshold of life's fiery furnace.

I Always Hated Being Chosen Last

> Success is counted sweetest by those
> who ne'er succeed.
> —Emily Dickinson

I always hated being chosen
last for childhood games.
The stigma of being uncoordinated
followed me for years until,
in an unfamiliar place, I put
down roots to make a new start.

Now I compete only upon my own
merits. Earlier biases against me
are forgotten in this survival
world called, earning a living.

However, when those fateful words,
"We have to let you go," come
condescendingly and easily
from emotionless, orchestrated lips,
despair knots the stomach and
disillusionment and anger consume.

Even being chosen last at baseball
or dodgeball cannot compare
to facing anxious stares from
a spouse and children at the news
of "offers of early retirement,"
"downsizing," or "outsourcing,"
today's let-them-eat-cake excuses.

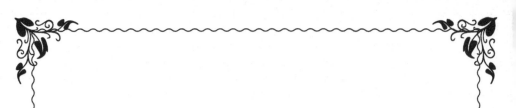

To enter again the resumé mill
with its countless rejections,
"overqualified," "underqualified,"
"We're not hiring," "We'll keep
your application on file for six months,"
"Thank you for applying, but . . ."
do not fill empty stomachs.

Today, my youngest awaits the
choice of MVP of his soccer game;
again, he is not chosen.
Repressing tears which came
easier in early childhood,
he turns to bury himself
in the treats and drinks
provided by the team mom.

I want to tell him to steel
himself for future disappointments,
but my tongue is stopped.

Only an encouraging hug is all
I must offer, as I knowingly
watch two yellow jackets compete
for his spilled orangeade.

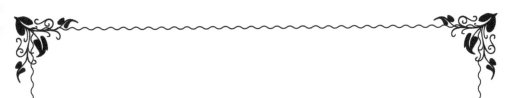

Bello es el canto

Bello es el canto caprichoso del pájaro solo
 en mañana agradable y tranquila sin viento inquieto.
De lejos llama a sus compañeros entonando
 canción feliz para invitarlos a probar bello día.

Levanto la cabeza y me despierto de este sueño
 deprimido, conocido como vida, a alcanzar
ver el origen oculto de animación tan dulce.

Agobiado con esta mi carga de apacentar
 rebaño rebelde y cabezudo, busco catársis
en música libre de la mañana generosa.

Sin embargo, un toque chocante a mi puerta disuelve
 la visión de serenidad fuera de mi ventana,
aunque cerca, me parece inasequible a esta hora
 llena de muchas preocupaciones inevitables.

Beautiful Is the Song . . .

The whimsical song of a lone bird is beautiful
   on a quiet morning without troublesome winds.
Intoning a happy song, it calls from afar to
   companions, inviting them to again taste of day.

I lift my head and wake from a depressing
   dream, called life, to attempt to determine
the hidden origin of such pleasing liveliness.

Weighed down with the burden of shepherding
   a rebellious and stubborn flock, I seek catharsis
in this spontaneous music of a congenial morning.

Yet, reality in a disturbing knock at my door
   dissolves the vision of serenity outside my window.
Even though close, it now seems unattainable
   at this hour full of inevitable preoccupations.

Amor fidel

—En memoria de mis abuelos

Nostaligia evocada por noche solitaria cuando
    ni se mueven las árboles, trae imagen de
un matrimonio en la oscuridad con manos
    enlazadas meciendo en sus mecedoras.

Todavía enamorados y contentos susurran
    su amor en vez de trompetearlo al mundo.

Pasado el tiempo de combatir contra los
    elementos para su propio sostén quedan
venerados por sus hijos ahora libres
    del nido y probando sus propias alas.

No tienen que expresar con palabras los
    sentimientos de ese momento, pero el mundo
envidioso los observa por medio del espejo
    de esta memoria y se para suspenso.

True Devotion

Nostalgia wells up within on a solitary night when
   even the trees do not move bringing back memories
of a devoted couple in tender twilight with hands
   intertwined and rocking together in their rocking chairs.

Still in love they are content to whisper their love for each
   other rather than trumpet it before the voyeuristic world.

Time has passed for them when they had to contend
   earnestly with the elements for their family's sustenance.

More than ever, they remain revered by their children, now
   liberated from the nest and testing their own unsure wings.

They do not have to express their love in words
   during these special interludes, but the envious
few who watch them by way of the enchanted
   mirror of memory, pause a moment in utter awe.

- In memory of my grandparents -

Nightly Vigils

The vigils we keep come alive in books and
   images on screen of campfires securing
the safety of those fortunate enough to sleep.

I often ponder over each unnerving scene
   asking what dangers lurk in the darkness
of each jungle, forest, or perilous minefield.

The anxiety and fear of designated watchmen
   as they bravely struggle with drowsiness leaning
on swords or guns poised against unseen
   enemies, lingers hauntingly in my memory.

But, morning again dawns relieving the watch
   as endurance is overcome with sleep, leaving
those secured during night to continue
   the many meaningless battles of day.

From my armchair strategically placed
   to witness a wayward's clandestine arrival,
I, too, endure my parental vigil with angst
   on many a sleepless night when the only
dreams are anxious hopes of a safe return.

Although the physical perils and enemies
   of today may not be as great as in the days
depicted in novels and war movies, my
   nightly task is yet as formidable as I try
to preserve with heart-rending anguish
   the spiritual safety of my prodigal.

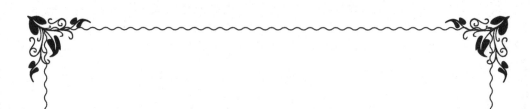

Presagio espejado en cielo azulado

La armonía y la paz de la naturaleza
espejada en el mero estanque del cielo
azul aquieta el vagabundo agitado
por los cargos pesados de subsistir.

A veces el hombre errante y solitario
se para triste a mirar y contemplarse
en ese estanque tranquilo y a preguntarse
el designio de esta vida trastornada.

Empero, del fondo de lo misterioso
firmamento resuena el eco asombroso
de aquella voz del tiempo desvaneciéndose
en estruendos de aquél reloj siempiterno
que presagia el juicio para esta existencia
en repiques espantosos y chocantes.

Omen on a Clear Day

The harmony and peace of nature
mirrored in the sky's blue lagoon
calms the agitated vagabond of
the heavy burdens of survival.

At times the errant and solitary man
sadly stops to look at himself
in this tranquil pool and asks himself
the purpose of this mad existence.

Yet, from the depths of the mysterious
firmament resounds the eerie echo
of the faraway voice of time disappearing
into the clamor of the everlasting clock
which foretells the end of existence
in the ghostly ringing of its chimes.

Two bronze images on horseback,
   one with head turned slightly
gazing intently at the other,
   as if engaged in conversation.

One can almost smell the late
   spring alfalfa and hear children
gleefully playing in the distance.

Lowing of cattle and nostalgic
   cowbells fade as the two figures
with melancholy contemplate
   one last time their beloved home.

Reluctantly, their horses carry
   them to inevitable incarceration
while they await another expected,
   erroneous, spiteful adjudication
which dolefully was not to be.

Evening gunshots shattered the
   deceptive serenity leaving their
followers and loved ones bereft
   of joy and hope, disconsolate in
mourning this tragic injustice.

Yet, consolation came in knowing
   that, even in death, these brothers
were not separated and the legacy
   they left could not be forgotten.

Now, the sun as a glorious backdrop
   emblazons the two silhouettes
crowning them with golden sunset.

The Abyss

When one in awe looks into the great
    abyss and the abyss looks back,
the stirrings of an unsettled universe
    reverberate throughout every sinew
of one's being, scanning for every flaw.

The cosmic mirror unveiled by this split-
    second encounter, through other worldly
eyes, affords only momentary glimpses of
    forever while tender mercy spares vulnerable
flesh and spirit immediate dissolution.

Only humble preparation by the casting off
    of all worldliness can one endure again
examination by this chasm, which may
    impart to the very core perfect revelation.

Image is being used by permission of NASA.

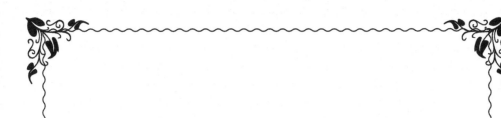

"Lollipops and Roses"

Remember when lollipops seemed so
  large and such a sumptuous treasure
to youthful eyes amazed at life's many
  wonders now ready to be experienced?

It was only yesterday when jump ropes
  and braids were exchanged for roses
and elegant prom dresses to explore,
  with apprehension, a world of emotions
unleashed with approaching maturity.

The roses have not been replaced as
  expressions of love, but have become
less frequent as the strain of routine life
  causes unintended neglect, distraction.

Yet, these wonderful memories, now
  archived in more mature hearts, can
be rekindled with a simple smile and
  a wink as reminders in later years of
those unforgettable lollipops and roses.

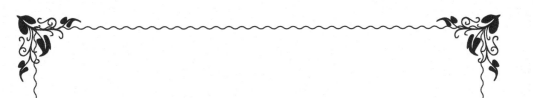

Enduring Choices

The gentle, alluring scent of a
    classic rose entices those insects
to its bloom while others, the more
    flamboyant ones, created by man's
design, lure other creatures
    through visual impressions.

We, like all living beings,
    face similar and difficult,
personal options and must
    exercise cautious judgment
when differentiating between
    the fleeting allure of man-made
titillations and the fulfilling
    gratification of enduring choices.

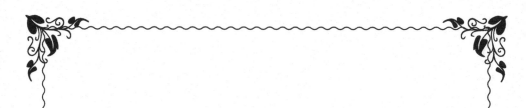

Aurora de febrero

En meditación profunda contemplo
horizonte de mañana iluminada,
aurora furtiva acechando las sombras
de noche para sofocarlas plenamente.

Una ave solitaria vuela lento encima
de árboles desnudos, ahora quietos,
sufriendo otro invierno indiferente.

Una ardilla hambrienta corre a locuras
entre rocas y zarzas para encontrar
pocos fragmentos de sostén ilusivo.

Paz reina por sólo un instante mientras
este mundo de insensatez se despierta
de la embriaguez de seguir el camino
que se lleva a desesperación y abulia.

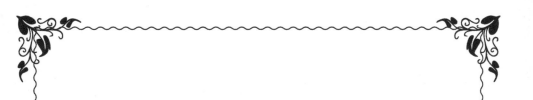

February Dawn

In deep meditation I muse upon
  the brilliant morning horizon when
secretive dawn stalks the shadows
  of night suffocating them completely.

A solitary bird flies slowly above
  the naked, quiet trees suffering
through another insensitive winter.

A hungry squirrel scurries among
  the rocks and bushes looking for
a few morsels of elusive sustenance.

Peace reigns only for an instant
  while this world of insensibility awakens
to the drunkenness of pursuing the
  path that leads to despair and abulia.

Las hojas de otoño

Las hojas, bailarinas de otoño,
* sin el color verde vibrante,*
ahora vestidas en diversas
* matices—moreno, amarillo y rojo,*
bailan al ritmo del viento frío,
* el presagio de invierno áspero,*
cuando toda naturaleza duerme
* esperando nueva luz fresca.*

Empujadas a tiempo de la música
* misteriosa de las brisas otoñales*
buscan refugio en los rincones
* escondidos donde pueden suspirar*
y empezar el proceso de degenerarse
* cubiertas en la opiata de nieve.*

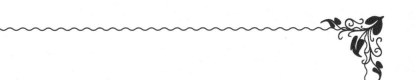

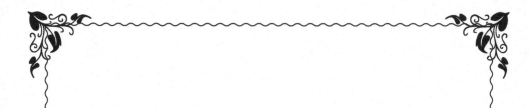

The Leaves of Autumn

Leaves, the ballerinas of autumn
    without the vibrant green of summer,
dressed in various colors: brown,
    yellow, orange, and red now dance to
the rhythm of a cold wind, the omen
    of harsh winter, when all nature sleeps
and dreams hoping for the promise
    of welcomed, refreshing light of spring.

Driven to the tempo of mysterious
    music of autumn breezes, the most
fortunate seek refuge in hidden
    corners where they can assuredly
rest and begin the process of decay
    gently nestled in the opiate of snow.

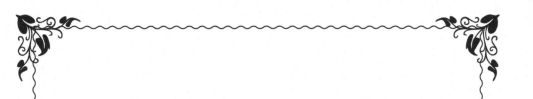

Cuando palabras no sirven

Las palabras nos abandonan en momentos
*   de tristeza cuando uno entre lágrimas trata*
de reconciliar la muerte de un bien amado.

El consuelo ofrecido es poca recompensa
*   por la profunda pérdida que se realiza*
en unas ondas de sollozos, melancolía.

La cicatriz dejada parece asquerosa;
*   mas, con el tiempo se ablanda hasta disolverse*
en aguas curativas de alivio anhelado,
*   pero queda grabada en memoria indeleble.*

Aunque descargado de la tristeza ancha
*   por ahora, sigue adelante contando*
el tiempo desde ese entierro pesaroso
*   cuando llegue aquella aurora prometida.*

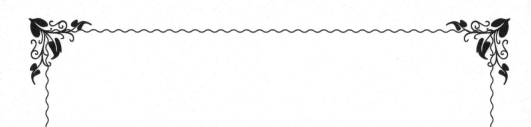

When Words Are Not Enough

Words abandon us in moments of sadness
　　and sorrow, when we try through many
tears to reconcile the passing of a loved one.

The hand of condolence is of little consequence
　　compared to the seemingly unfathomable loss
we experience in waves of sobs and melancholy.

The scar left behind seems grotesque, yet
　　with time it becomes smooth and dissolves
in healing waters of welcomed comfort, but
　　will ever remain engraved upon our memories.

Although unburdened of deep sorrow now,
　　we will continue to count time forward from
that woeful day until, in praise, we joyfully
　　celebrate the arrival of that promised aurora.

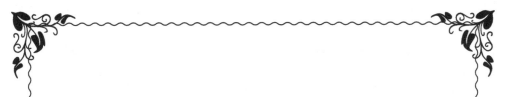

Through the Nightly Looking Glass of Rustling Leaves

(A Summer Concerto)

There are melodies and pictures hidden
    in memories which languish only to be
revisited in waves of melancholy, like tides
    rising and receding from the seashore.

Buried within each sinew of yesterday and
    emerging marrow of tomorrow lies elusive
happiness mixed with ever-present sadness,
    both waiting to be awakened in harmonies
of major and minor chords performed by
    the concert master's fine-tuned instrument.

Every heartbeat and each tick of the clock
    echo loudly in those mysteriously quiet
chambers where only those washed in
    the blood of experience and pain, enter
naked into the special sanctuary leaving
    all guile behind, like Nathanael seated
under the fig tree waiting to drink living
    water and worship with grateful tears.

There it is that knightly vanity and assumed
    sanctity disappear in the baptism by fire,
shedding the old and emerging from
    our cocoons into the promise of new life.

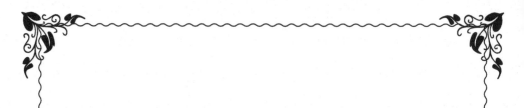

Shenandoah

Hearts heavy with poignant memories
   of long-ago places and happy moments
coalesce with melodic, mystical strains
   of enchanted strings which renew longing
for renewal in fountains of calming waters,
   being immersed gently to loose the sting
of those lost days of youth, never to return.

When least expected those past, but
   not forgotten, memories will in waves wash
over the wounded mired in the commonplace,
   liberating a torrent of pent-up tears that
cleanse the cobwebbed soul with renewed
   hope for better days when the peaceful
waters of Shenandoah are seen again.

El mármol frío

La tentación de desasir pasión oculta
encerrada en esta pluma dándome mareo,
hasta en solitud me reviento en mil pedazos
insignificantes esparciéndose al cielo.

Pero, razón indiferente me restringe
y fuerte me castiga y enseña disciplina.

De esta batalla se brotan versos ya crudos
pero después forjados con sudor y lágrimas
en aquel horno cruel adonde se disuelven
orgullo, ostentación y vanagloria loca.

Más, llega momento feo en lo cual como autómoton
grabo, sin pensar, muchas palabras torcidas.

Así es con los escultores ya desilusionados
luchan con el mármol frío para crear algo admirable.

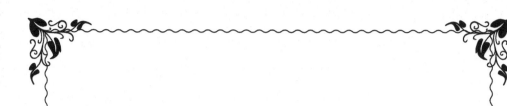

Cold Marble

The temptation to release the pent-up
passions from this pen, makes me dizzy,
until, in the eerie quiet I explode into
insignificant pieces scattered on the sky.

Yet indifferent reason restrains me and
strongly chastises, teaching discipline.

From this battle spring unrefined verses
which later are forged with sweat and
tears in that cruel furnace where pride,
ostentation and vanity disappear.

Yet, the moment will come when as a robot
I will carve these contorted words in iron, just
as a sculptor disillusioned with the cold marble
he is given to attempt another admirable creation.

Mañana de verano

Ligera es la mera mañana de verano
   antes de venir esa energía intensa del sol
cuando solamente mis amigos plumados
   rompen el silencio con sus cantos de gozo.

Ondas de calma me inundan en tales horas
   calmando corazón tierno, ahora agitado
preparándome para otro día arrebatado.

Solamente mañanas de las Sierra escapan
   vientos de la tarde, incómodos, que molestan
aun los monjes en su contemplación más honda.

Resignado y con tristeza me despido de
   la aurora a empezar este trabajo mundano.

Mas, para librarme del tedio diario, sólo
   reflejo en mañanas hermosas de verano.

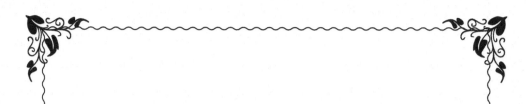

A Summer's Morning

Tender is the early summer morning before
   the arrival of the intense energy of the sun,
when only my friends, the lonely birds,
   break the silence with their joyful songs.

In those hours, waves of calm cover me
   placating my delicate, yet uneasy heart
preparing me for the day that will come.

Only mornings in the Sierras escape
   the pesky winds of day which vex even
the monks in their deepest contemplation.

Sadly and reluctantly, I must bid farewell
   to the aurora and begin my daily tasks.

Yet, to free myself from this tedium, I simply
   reflect on a beautiful summer sunrise.

Tributo a *Les Misérables*

*Las aflicciones de los humildes de la tierra
indiferente claman al cielo por justicia
en medio de tristeza profunda y miseria
encubierta en trapos y pies descalzados.*

*Por sólo tratar de vivir, uno está condenado por
haber robado un pan para los hijos de su hermana
hambrientos, más relegados a ser únicamente
ratones de la calle rascando la existencia.*

*Ahora, dichoso es el joven que sea rescatado
en los brazos de su héroe doblado e implorando
la consciencia suprema le dé al desfortunado
alivio en la mansión preparada para los
esclavos en la carne y acepte su ofrenda,
un corazón quebrantado y un espíritu contrito.*

Tribute to *Les Misérables*

The afflictions of all the humble of an
indifferent earth cry to heaven for justice
from their profound sadness and misery
mirrored in their rags and no shoes.

For merely having tried to survive, one is
condemned for stealing a loaf of bread
for his sister's children, now consigned to
the streets like rats eking out an existence.

A prayer for a fortunate youth rescued in
the arms of our hero who kneels, imploring
heaven to exchange himself for the youth
and a mansion prepared for the slaves
of this wretched flesh and accept an offer
of his broken heart and a contrite spirit.

Neglected Corners

In our neglected corners
  many unhappy, suppressed
feelings are hurriedly tossed
  to collect dust, to decay.

Some become dust themselves,
  but others multiply as mold or
moss turning ugly, menacing,
  requiring painful excision.

If left undisturbed these sly
  gremlins with untamed ferocity
may lash out until even their
  creators suffer irreparable injury
leaving behind chaos and hurt.

Warmth and tenderness can
  pacify their savage nature as
kind words, too, melt years of
  festering into healing honey.

Yet, eventually inured and
  hardened even Pollyanna
shrinks from sunshine if
  not nurtured by soothing
rain and friendly soil.

If we continue to conveniently
  forget and bury each sensitive
impression, we are condemned
  to wallow in Darwin's jungle
with only the insensitive beasts.

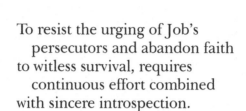

To resist the urging of Job's
    persecutors and abandon faith
to witless survival, requires
    continuous effort combined
with sincere introspection.

When finally the offended
    and offender are reconciled
in forgiveness' unconditional
    embrace, then prodigal and
faithful may live in harmony
    and bury all animosity, where
light of morning never again
    will touch it to revive man's
tendencies toward inhumanity.

Only heaven's intervention
    and genuine tears of contrition
falling upon our burial
    places can safely unlock
the moldering vestiges
    of unresolved conflicts,
dissolving them wondrously
    into clear, purified water
which bathes the furrowed
    brow and lifts the careworn,
now tempered, like steel,
    to endure future assaults
from inevitable adversity.

Divine tenderness will then
    sweep away the cobwebs from
our darkness, which we have
    previously ignored, miraculously
purging our neglected corners.

Secret Garden

When the rush of day and
    each tick of the clock become
unbearable, I retire to my
    secret garden where the calm
of trickling waters lulls my
    consciousness and I daydream
while unwitting nature quietly
    weaves her mosaic in time.

If I gaze long enough into
    its lotus-laden pool, I can
sense its essence invading
    my being, until I become
wholly part of this peaceful
    corner of the universe.

Thresholds

Each threshold we cross over
  brings more freedom, independence
from the source of our sustenance,
nurturing.

Graduation from dependence
  upon our mother's milk to solid
foods is always a monumental
  step we all take to reach another
rung on the uncertain ladder to
maturity.

Our first steps, graduations from
  schools, universities, become
more milestones toward self-
fulfillment.

Yet, that fretful journey from
  caterpillar to emerging, frail
moth is fraught with perils
  leaving success to fateful
destiny.

Only the hoarfrosts of aging
  seem to restrain our illusive
independence, reminding us
  upon whom we are all still
dependent.

Santuario atesorado

Pocas veces puedo invitar visitas
al santuario mío donde mis deseos
mas profundos quedan cerrados
para liberación en día memorable.

Muchos saben que no deben entrar
en mi santuario a ruídos porque es
tierra santa y me dejan en paz
para comunicarme con mi destino.

Los que por desgracia interrumpen
mi solitud comprenden de inmediato
la indiscreción que han cometido,
no por mi enojo ni por impaciencia,
sino por sentirse ajenos e incómodos
en la presencia de inspiración desnuda.

No quiero salir de allí cuando se toca
el teléfono como insecto nocivo indicando
que el mundo me llama a volver
a la realidad de luchar para sobrevivir.

Cuando me meto una vez mas en
el asilo guardado para mis pensamientos
privados y reservados, respiro
aire fresco y recojo esfuerzo para
aguantar otro día con sus desdichas.

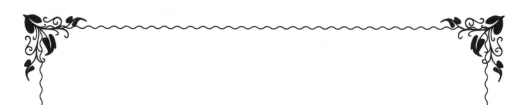

Treasured Sanctuary

Seldom do I invite visitors into
   my sanctuary where my deepest
desires remain locked awaiting
   liberation on a memorable day.

Many know that they should enter
   quietly, since where they stand is
holy ground and they must leave me
   in peace to confer with my destiny.

Those who unfortunately interrupt
   my solitude comprehend immediately
the indiscretion they have committed,
   not because of anger nor impatience,
but they are sure to feel uncomfortable
   in the presence of naked inspiration.

I dislike leaving when the telephone rings
   like a pesky insect reminding me the world
has called piercing my solitude, signaling
   my return to the unwanted battle of survival.

When I confine myself one more time
   in this asylum, storage for my private
and reserved thoughts, I take in its
   fresh air to muster the strength to with-
stand another day with its misfortunes.

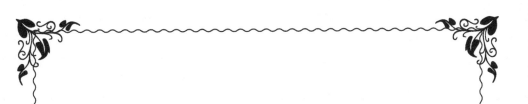

Unanswered

The question mark your name
evokes awakens unrest, tossing,
turning, leading to pressing inquiry.

No one I know can recall your final
days, only your parents can
remember, but they will not say,
avoiding recurrent pain each
time someone like me asks.

The memories of our shared youth,
like your energetic smile begin to dim,
but never completely disappear
remaining as haunting impressions,
persistent, fleeting mirages
in this desert of loneliness.

I long to greet you as before, but,
your father's words, "he's now able
to rest," give him solace, serving
only to leave me empty, hungry
for a period to your existence.

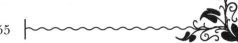

In Contemplation of Winter's Tranquility

Peacefulness in light-falling snow
   covers a distraught landscape
withdrawn within itself, awaiting
   sleepily the merciful touch of
spring's warming breezes and
   stirrings of an awakened earth.

Only in such rare moments of
   rapt contemplation of winter's
tranquility, does the universe
   in a snowflake loom large to
the perceptive eye carefully
   prepared for this inspiration.

Now, with snowy brow I too,
   await gentle warming breezes.

Meditation on Seeing *Phantom of the Opera*

Not far from most theater districts, panderers,
    homeless, those asking for another dollar
for one more shot of whiskey mingle with
    pleasure-seekers and addicts while patrons
of the stage hurry toward a reserved seat.

One self-assured couple in haste brusquely
    reject a disgusting offer of a bottle from one
down, but determined to begin then to resist
    his ever-present, impish "angel of music."

Comfortably situated and in anticipation,
    from clever advertising, another audience
is not disappointed from the curtain's
    rising until its final setting in mystery.

To witness through hypnotic music, Christine's
    enslavement to her monstrous, alluring master
conjures feelings of pity, yet gratitude in many
    supposedly safe from the enticements of today.

Christine's struggle to resist her specter's seduction
    finally ends as atonement embodied in Raoul, her
brave knight, rescues her from her enigmatic host.

But one final ambivalent attraction takes her
    swiftly to that former dungeon to return the ring
which bound her to her angel of night.

The echo of applause dies quickly as all exit
    onto those streets of reality, but the catharsis,
intended by ingenious composers and producers,
    on some is lost, while those truly touched by this
depiction of art in life, make a resolve, like Christine,
    to leave behind the phantoms which haunt us all.

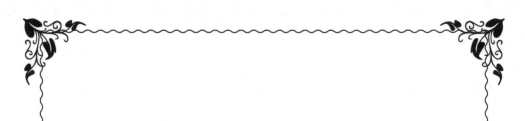

Molly

Even the clouds seem to know how
   I feel today as they gray the blue
sky with oppressive sadness.

The nearly spent leaves of August
   welcome a cooler breeze bringing
hints of autumn and soothing rains.

Watching her pain-ridden body
   struggle to survive against the wind
hoping for another breath, which
   would not come, was agony for me;
yet, I knew the end was near.

The good-bye through veiled tears
   left my heart in pieces leaving only
sweet memories to melt the clouds.

Primavera inolvidable

Inconscientes de la mera primavera
aves a nido, con ruido agradable,
pipian a una brisa antojadiza
y se recogen a esperar mientras
las querellas de unos arrendajos,
peleando entre sí por migajas
dejadas al lado del sendero,
disturban esta escena hermosa.

Resignado me vuelvo triste a lo
cotidiano sin el ánimo de continuar
con dedicación a la tarea de ser.

Otra vez enjaulado yo, sin poder
olvidar primavera, el azul del
cielo espacioso reflejado en
mi computadora, me distrae.

Lo dejo y salgo fuera cuando me
presenta panorama del arco iris
en las flores de abril desplegadas
a la vista aborrida con gris del
invierno que me parecía incesante.

Unos vientos, ahora suaves, no
tempestuosos, mecen la cuna
de la temporada al ritmo etéreo,
y duermo sin preocupaciones
en los brazos de esta belleza.

Unforgettable Spring

Unaware of the arrival of spring
   birds in the nest with pleasing
noises, chirp to the whimsical
   breeze and withdraw to await
sustenance, while the quarreling
   of mockingbirds, fighting among
themselves for the crumbs left at
   the side of the pathway, disturb
this unforgettably artistic scene.

With resignation, I sadly return to
   my daily tasks without enthusiasm
to continue with dedication to living.

The expansive blue sky reflected
   in my computer distracts me,
as I am once again in my cage
   without the power to forget spring.

I leave all behind and go outside
   where a panorama of rainbow colors
of the flowers of April is displayed
   to my view, now tired of the gray of
winter which has seemed so endless.

The breeze, now soft, rocks the cradle
   of the season to an extraterrestrial rhythm,
and I sleep without worries wrapped in
   the arms of spring's exquisite beauty

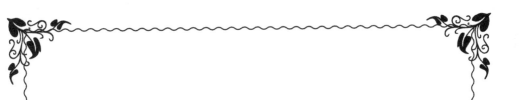

Libertad

Cuando escoje el cielo ponerse
   menos que azul, claro todos los
políticos, eruditos y científicos no
   pueden mandarlo volverse azul.

También, aunque me echan en
   una jaula con cadenas modernas
llamadas softwere y hardware, no
   pueden quitarme el espíritu libre
ni hacerme callar los pensamientos
   vivos que me preservan del tedio
inventado que llaman, "modernismo."

Sólo al quebrar estos grillos que me
   restringen, me volaré emancipado
con águilas al sol y veré el mundo
   ahora hecho cristal para revelar
a los videntes el propósito de ser.

Liberation

When the sky chooses to be less
   than clear blue, the politicians,
the erudite and scientists cannot
   command it to return to blue.

Likewise, even though they throw me
   into a cage with these modern chains
called software and hardware, they
   cannot deny freedom to my spirit nor
can they silence my resonating thoughts
   which save me from this tedium
invented in the guise of "modernism."

Only in breaking out of these fetters
   which restrain can I now, emancipated,
soar with eagles to the sun and glimpse
   a world now turned to crystal revealing
to the seers the purpose of life.

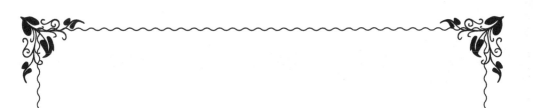

Morning Walk

The path seems somehow
   much longer today even
though we always go this way.

Max knows but cannot say
   what we both are feeling.

The cacophony of morning
   birds awakens my consciousness
with their natural harmony.

This everyday awareness
   opens discoveries hidden
in the chants of dawn that
   continue ringing in my head.

We communicate without words;
   I know the trail, Max does too.

Today the familiar feels
   strange since with age
I stop to rest much more.

Autumn Miracle

Hope and faith hidden in the last
   rosebud of autumn shines radiantly
in the rising sun of morning when an
   indifferent world ignores the brilliance
displayed above.
                  Leaves are quiet as
   a silent stream in adoration of the miracle
of dawn, a secret opportunity to breathe
   freely, to taste beauty concealed to those
who choose to be blind.
                  The mirror in
   a serene mountain lake reflects a calm sky
just like a quiet sea that awaits the storm
   which stalks the perplexed vagabond to
drown him in its menacing deep.
                  Then all nature
gratefully kneels to plead for deliverance.

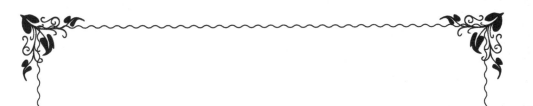

Sonata de la noche

Profundidad nocturna habla del abismo
en susurros al principio, más aumentando
despacio hasta estallarse de lo mas alto
en voz baja y recia a amonestar al mundo
liviano, embriagado en narcisismo y orgullo.

Tal pesadilla achecha tranquilidad
disfrazada en forma del fantasma infame
que molestaba la ópera ficticiosa,
captando cada ser débil y engañado
por las artimañas de la noche sutil.

Con resolución e impaciencia infantil
el hombre extraviado amenaza los cielos
con puño exigiendo respuesta inmediata
que solo viene, después de tribulación,
en forma de voz pequeña y penetrante.

Night Sonata

From the great expanse, the depths of night
speak in whispers at first, then slowly
crescendoing until it explodes from
the heights in a loud, deep voice warning
a blithe world drunken with narcissistic pride.

Such a nightmare, subtly disguised as
the infamous phantom, that haunted
the fictional opera house, stalks serenity
attracting each weak and deceived
person by the wiles of furtive night.

With resolution and infantile impatience
one unfortunate soul threatens the heavens
with a clenched fist demanding an immediate
response, which only will come after much
tribulation, in the form of a still, small voice.

Passage to Infamy

—A visit to Washington, DC's, Holocaust Museum

The unthinkable terror of Auschwitz
confined in claustrophobic cells looms
ever larger with every measured step
through corridors lined with photographs
of those extinguished by blind fanaticism.

By design like innumerable cattle thronging
toward an unknown fate, lines of curiosity
seekers mill through succeeding revelations
of inhumanity, crossing that inevitable
threshold from naïveté and indifference
to the world of stark comprehension.

Each display reverberates with unconsolable
cries against injustices which can never be
reconciled by past or present political impotence.

Maps and charts present a methodical march
of genocide inflamed by perceived racial
superiority disguised as zealousness.

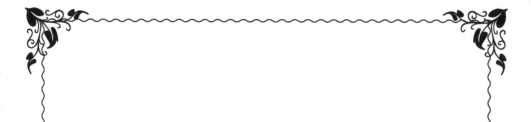

Discarded shoes covered with ashes spewed
from ignominious furnaces lie ominously
silent in heaps behind fences preventing
their irreverent disturbance by sadistic
collectors of sensational memorabilia.

No less unsettling are locks of shorn hair
alongside bales of hair ravaged in mass
from the unsuspecting, dutifully entering
austere chambers fitted with death-spitting
spigots disguised as showers ostensibly
to rid the unwary of unwanted vermin.

The vision of such atrocities is surpassed
only by haunting voices of survivors preserved
to recount abuse, depravation, suffering.

The realizations engendered by the visual
images raise their heads as hideous nightmares
preserved to pique even consciences seared
by selfish youth veneered with indifference.

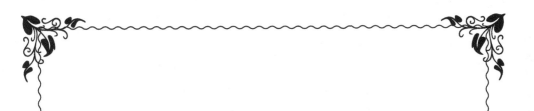

Repulsion comes even to those inured by
previous wars, after peering over cement
walls made to hide from tender feelings
human experiments couched in scientific
learning to enhance further warfare.

A tower of photos discovered in the remains
of a community obliterated from history,
as if instantaneously, portrays hatred
telegraphed from the eyes of invaders as
evil projectiles to immobilize resistance.

As disgust merges into feelings of
helplessness and complete abandonment,
the depiction of those last days of pain
changes all into momentary hope
when films of soldiers from the hammer
and sickle empire liberate the emaciated
thousands nearly bereft of body and soul.

Only those who have steeled themselves
in years of bigotry and apathy emerge
unchanged into the light chamber of liberation
where they pensively pause to reflect
smugly with gratitude having been spared.

Yet, those truly altered by travel
through another dimension of human
feeling struggle through a curtain
of tears leaving one, lone candle
to reflect the totality of this infamy.

> (Written on the fiftieth anniversary of the
> liberation of Auschwitz.)

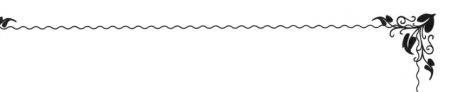

Nocturno español II

El espíritu y belleza de España
   se despliega en el ritmo del flamenco,
espejo del ánimo y ardor latino,
   incorporado en esas castañetas
y las máscaras de los bailadores.

En el fuego y las piruetas se trata
   de hacerse regocijar esta alma
triste al pensar en la gloria perdida
   que gozaba España en los días pasados
de armadas, reyes y conquistadores.

Se fluyen las faldas y capas rojas
   a la música encantada y repleta,
evocando siluetas de arte pura
   simbolizada en muñecas giradas
por adonises escultos, gentiles.

Con la última inclinación y la caída
   del talón me despiertan de este sueño
a esa realidad que siempre me acecha;
   mas, guardo una chispa de esta hermosura
para inspiración futura en días ásperos.

Spanish Nocturne II

The spirit and beauty of Spain is
    manifested in the rhythm of the flamenco,
the mirror of Latin verve and passion,
    which is embodied in the castanets,
costumes and masks of the dancers.

With the fire and pirouettes the saddened
    soul attempts to rejoice, but is overcome
with the contemplation of the now lost
    glory that once was Spain of the days
of armadas, kings, and conquistadores.

The skirts and capes flow quickly
    to the haunting music replete with
the vision of pure art embodied in
    dolls spinning under the arms of
the sculpted and lively Adonises.

With the final bow and the curtain falling
    I am awakened from this artistic dream
to reality which continues to stalk me;
    yet, I treasure a spark of this beauty for
future inspiration on inevitable dark days.

A Rose Garden Reply to Darwin

I have struggled against
    Darwinian forces to cultivate
beauty in arid Sierran soil.

Each blossom, though smaller
    than those from richer earth,
is more precious by far.

One particular bloom eclipses
    all others unfolding in splendor,
soft, luminescent pink, with
    an unforgettable fragrance
which pervades summer's air.

This season is the last for this,
    my favorite, ailing and delicate.

It will succumb to aphids, wood
    borers that attack its weaknesses
daily, in spite of dusts I administer
    faithfully with Hippocratic concern.

Soon, I will no longer see my
    favorite, nor bask in its radiance,
yet I can only console myself
    knowing that its memorable
essence will forever be indelibly
    etched on my immortal memory.

Poesía

At last the floodgates have been
    opened again with words spewing
forth unorganized, twisted, contorted,
    yet filled with sentiment to be felt only
by one who chooses the least-worn path.

The task of aligning these fragile
    meanings into lasting treasures
furrows many a brow and ages
    a feeling heart yearning to hear again
each unleashed nuance and harmony.

Emotional orations and pleadings
    serve nothing to corral untamed
words into meaningful impressions
    which, in truth, cannot compare
to those that cannot be written.

Reflections on *Berceuse*
by Jean Sibellius

Concentric rings, reflections of immortality
in a secluded forest pool, slowly dissipate into
blackness of night, and resound throughout
universal stillness sinking deeply into those
hearts prepared for immeasurable joy.

Healing tears of gratitude briefly blur the memory
etched by enchanting strains surging from each
epiphanic moment which comforts like soft
blankets, shields from uncertainties of living.

Inevitable sadness returns when melodies
end and the symphonic grandeur ceases,
leaving only thirst for the next manifestation
mercifully bestowed upon unworthy mankind
cradled in the awesome immensity of eternity.

Transcendent Music

Longings for eternity encircle
   every thought and vision from
syncopated rhythms of haunting
   music which endures in memory
long after its final moving chords
   disappear into the humdrum
oblivion of monotony disguised
   as salvation through acquisition.

Yet, like the sun's rays awaken
   the world to one more radiant day,
music's moving, but gentle caress
   from the baton of one prepared to
inspire can elevate a soul mired
   in self-pity and discouragement.

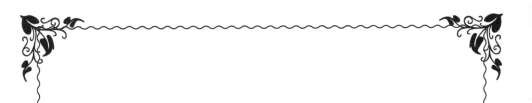

Una visita a la pirámide *Luxor*

Las esferas que creamos nos esclavizan
en cámaras vacías, pero resonantes
con voces de los ancianos que allí andaban
en una búsqueda infinita y enigmática
para encontrar la felicidad efímera.

Sólo el soberbio ignora las instrucciones
hieroglíficas inscritas con muchas
lágrimas, sudor y sangre inestimable
de generaciones difuntas gritando
ahora amonestaciones a los sordos.

Con asombro se contempla estas escenas
mientras cautivado en un nave encantado.

Al salir a la atmósfera carnavalesca
pronto se olvida el mensage de las edades.

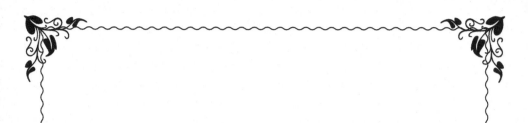

A Visit to the *Luxor* Pyramid

The various spheres which we create
hypnotize us in those empty rooms, which
resonate with voices of the ancients who
roamed there in the endless, enigmatic
search for evasive, ephemeral happiness.

Only the proud ignore the instructions
in hieroglyphics inscribed with many
tears, sweat, and the precious blood of
generations now defunct and trying to
warn those who, by choice, may be deaf.

With great wonderment one considers such
scenes while captive in an enchanted boat.

Yet, leaving this carnival-like atmosphere most
deliberately forget the lessons from past ages.

Sports' Mating Dance

The mating dance of feathered
   athletes after displayed prowess,
spoils the achievement from
   "showboating" antics to attract
a hoped for showering of accolades
   from conceited commentators,
all this in the revered pursuit of
   seductive, elusive fame and fortune.

The Gettysburg Address

Memorable brevity is a gift
that many writers and orators
never achieve, because
seductive words continue
to stoke inflated egos.

A Caprice

The mystery of grandma's kitchen
   alchemy remains buried with her,
although her daughters in vain
   attempted to duplicate those
delicacies only she could concoct.

She always saved a bowl of soup
   or, as I recall, a secreted slice of
meat or a piece of pastry for me.

As a child, I always raved about
   her cooking, perhaps that is why
she seemed to favor me; at least,
   my ego wanted it so, in spite of the
protests of my siblings and cousins.

Unfortunately, I guess I will never know.

Imaginación suelta

Me asombro con boca abierta al contemplar
cielos desenrollados y desplegados en un
panorama de estrellas, planetas, y lunas.

En este éxtasis suelto la mente, la única
parte de mi ser que es capaz de salir
libre a explorar los universos cerrados
en imaginación sagrada, no obstante,
los deberes mundanos me llaman con
choque duro a esta realidad calderoniana.

Más, hago la lucha para preservar sólo
unas moléculas para otros momentos
asombrosos cuando otra vez penetro detrás
del velo a ver las perplejidades de tantos
océanos y átomos de esta existencia.

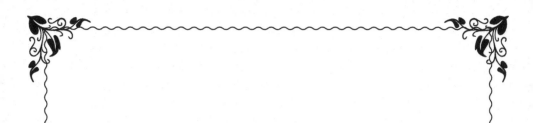

Imagination Unleashed

In contemplation of the heavens, I stand in
awe as they are unrolled and displayed before
me in a panorama of stars, planets, and moons.

In this hypnotic trance I liberate my mind,
the only part of me that can travel freely
to explore universes locked in my sacred
imagination; nonetheless, mundane
duties abruptly call me back from my
cherished reverie to this Calderonian reality.

Still, I must fight to preserve only a few
molecules for another inspirational moment
when once again I am allowed to penetrate
the veil to see the perplexities of the many
oceans and atoms of this amazing existence.

Reconciliando a morte

A manhã seguinte não hà felicidade
depois da morte de uma pessoa muita amada.

Parece-me que outra aurora não pasa-se mais
pensando que uma vida dissipa tão fácil.

Eu não sinto-o mais por razão da ruptura
de meu coracão que era como cristal antes.

Não mais brilha este sol, salvo escurece-se ainda
o meio-dia aos meus olhos cegos por o pesar.

As tristes lágrimas vertidas desfacem-se
nos rios fluindo aos grandes mares tranqüilizantes
para os aflitos que, com fe, recebem paz.

Agora vou ao altar de manhã a colocar
minha alma acima, oferecendo-a como dádiva
aos cegos que não podem acreditar num céu.

Reconciling Death

There is no happiness the morning after
   the death of a loved one; it just seems
that another sunrise will never occur
   again since a life can end so easily.

I do not feel any more because of this
   broken heart that was like crystal before.

Now even the sun does not shine, while noonday
   seems dark to my eyes now blinded by sorrow.

Tears shed in sadness disappear into rivers
   flowing into those great tranquil seas from which
the afflicted, through faith, may receive peace.

For this, I must now go to the altar of morning,
   placing my soul there as an offering—a gift to
those who are blind and cannot believe in heaven.

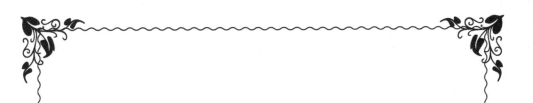

Canto a la vejez

La caída lenta de hojas de otoño
reflejan el humor de una tierra
harta con disipaciones tantas
del verano muriéndose a pasos.

Por fin duerme el mundo tiritado
en este viento áspero del otoño,
descargándose en sueño sereno
de todos los excesos del verano.

Como el otoño anhela el reposo,
yo pateo las hojas en la acera
contemplando llegada de invierno
tremendo con canas y dolores.

Mas, sigo resignado y agradecido
por vida amplia de flores y cascadas.

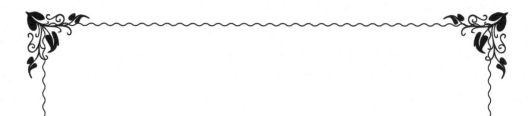

Song of Aging

The leaves of autumn falling gently
  reflect the somber mood of tired
earth inebriated by the rhythms of
  dissipate summer slowly dying.

Resolutely, the world shivers in
  harsh winds of fall and sleeps
with peaceful dreams to unburden
  itself of the excesses of summer.

As autumn yearns for rest, I shuffle
  through the leaves while contemplating
with awe the arrival of winter with
  its inevitable pains and graying hair.

Yet I am content, grateful for a life filled
  with beautiful flowers and waterfalls.

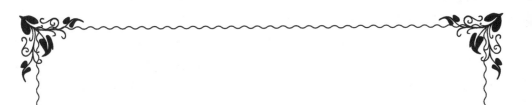

La Cumbre de *Kilimanjaro*

*La jornada árdua de esta vida
    a través del desierto formidable
oprime alma dedicada a buscar
    la belleza y majestad de existencia.*

*Los oases infrecuentes no satisfacen;
    sólo la vista del agua del mar,
la meta fijada para él que busca,
    traerá la felicidad deseada que
puede elevar hombre desconsolado
    a la cima áspera de Kilimanjaro.*

*De evitar una caída calamitosa
    se esfuerza uno fervientemente
descender del monte sagrado para
    incitar a otros alcanzar la cumbre.*

The Heights of *Kilimanjaro*

The arduous journey of life across this
    formidable desert discourages even
those dedicated souls who search for
    the beauty and majesty of existence.

Infrequent oases do not satisfy, only
    the sight of ocean's life-giving water,
the fixed goal for him who searches,
    brings desired happiness and will
elevate disconsolate man in his quest
    to attain the harsh crest of *Kilimanjaro*.

Avoiding inevitable perils requires earnest
    dedication and inner strength to descend that
sacred mountain, as encouragement to those
    who follow in their attempts to scale its heights.

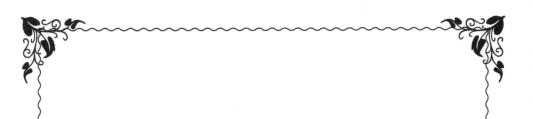

A Remembrance from *Les Misérables*

Boisterous laughter amid friendly cheers
from poignant remembrances of happier
days gone by, become only whispers on
doleful winds chilling a soul filled with grief
for those lost in seemingly futile battles
against injustices of an upside-down world.

Each familiar, beloved face marches past
in this vision of one miraculously spared
the fate of those who sacrificed themselves
that he might live to see one more day.

Still, those empty chairs and empty tables
will forever remind not just him, but also all
who have achieved true liberation from man's
inhumanity, of the cost of such freedom and
with tears etch sincere gratitude into hearts
forever changed by such hallowed memories.

Singing Shenandoah

Those who live music
    commence nostalgic, yet
melancholy whisperings
    of eternity encrypted
on atoms of everyman's
    tears which stream into
torrents of grief, longing,
    joy, elation, anxiety.

Each unforgettable strain
    disappears on the whimsical
wind and is soon extinguished,
    extinct for a seemingly long
season patiently awaiting
    another magical intonation.

About the Author

The author was born in Logan, Utah and raised in Cornish, Utah. He currently resides in Carson City, Nevada and has been a resident of Nevada for over 32 years. He married Carolyn, his wife, in 1970. The following year he graduated with a Bachelor of Arts from Utah State University in Spanish with minors in Music, English and German. He speaks and reads four languages: English, Spanish, Portuguese and German in that order of fluency with reading and speaking some French and Italian. He received a Juris Doctor from Brigham Young University in 1981. The author began writing poetry while in college. His hobbies include poetry, literature, gardening, music, singing and directing church choirs. He has five children and twelve grandchildren.